MW00988273

YOU'RE G~~~~~ ~~~ ~~~:

Harrowing Tales of Herpetology

Mark Ferdinand

YOU'RE GONNA' GET BIT!
Harrowing Tales of Herpetology
By
Mark Ferdinand

Copyright © 2016 by Mark Ferdinand
markferdinandbooks@gmail.com

All rights reserved. No part of this publication may be reproduced, stored in a retrieval system, or transmitted, in any form or by any means, electronic, mechanical, photocopying, recording or otherwise, without the prior permission of the copyright owner.

ISBN-13: 978-1530932399
ISBN-10: 1530932394

Mark Ferdinand is also the author of the autism adventure novel, Fortune on the Spectrum.

"Thank you for the work you do, Doctor."

"I'm not a doctor, but you're welcome."

Contents

Part I

A Place to Hunt

The red spitting cobra just looked at me and stared. It was one foot away from my face and I had surprised it as much as it had surprised me. Everything about this morning was normal and mundane, but in this situation I found myself in, all was highly out of place.

Close calls were nothing new in my time dealing with reptiles and amphibians. Some were more dangerous than others. I like to think I learned something from each one, but these are soulless and often unpredictable beings I deal with. Anything can happen.

I don't even keep many animals at home anymore. My days of being blindly obsessed with reptiles and amphibians are somewhat behind me. I now settle for one sixty-gallon tank in the living room that has a small ecosystem of fish, newts and frogs in it. Yes I still enjoy upsetting the modern purists in small ways!

My interest in animals started early as it does with countless children. I longed for the first time that I could visit the zoo and my first visit to see dinosaurs at the museum. I was fortunate to be raised on weekend visits to the mountains at the family cabin. Here I could stalk and capture critters to my heart's content.

In this area we had *Lithobates pipiens*, formerly known as *Rana pipiens* (Yeah just when I had a handle on the scientific name someone had to go and change it). We had leopard frogs, OK?

Also prevalent were *Thamnophis radix*. It took me a while to research which exact species of garter snake we had in my area growing up. See how passionate I am about such things? I finally settled on the Plains Garter Snake.

These two herps kept me busy for the first six years of my life. I started to get bored of them though. They became old hat to me. You always want what you don't have, and I wanted a turtle.

I became obsessed with turtles. I checked out every book on turtle topics at the library. My mother recognized my interest in them and bought me more books and more turtle knick-knacks to put on my shelf, but there was no actual turtle.

Turtles were not found at the high elevation that our weekend getaway was. I looked at the field guide maps and they showed that no less than three types of turtles could be found in that part of the state. Liars!

I needed to find a turtle. Fake turtles and turtles in books just weren't cutting it anymore.

The mountains were proving fruitless, so I needed to search in low country.

Our home was near the foothills of Northern Colorado. There were ponds there that one could explore, but none were close to my house. At one point a family friend took us to Miller Park and Miller Pond where a turtle was found by a group of older boys, but I was not old enough to remember much about the outing. I sure remember the turtle!

As I got a bit older, I got more mobile with the help of a Huffy bicycle and the freedom that kids in the summers of the 70's and 80's enjoyed. "Be back before dark" was the only rule at that time.

Unfortunately there was no Google Maps or any easy way to find ponds and streams and the like. Local knowledge was not very productive on "turtle ponds". We would have to go by rumor and legend. Only a very small elite handful of older kids shared in my interest, and most of them would safeguard any secrets they had of such places.

I finally had an "in" when my older brother started hanging out with a guy from a neighborhood a few miles away. They both liked playing the drums and the two of them were able to assemble an entire set with the equipment they owned put together. Each had one drum stick as I recall, drum rock legends have started this way I'm certain.

The friend was named Dave. I think you will find that a few guys attached to my stories were named "Dave". In some cases I am withholding the actual name of a person, but at very least the real individual has a one-syllable name. Either way, "Dave" is a solid name for a guy, and a perfectly believable name for a guy that is in to herps.

In addition to playing the drums and aspiring to rock legendry, Dave was a guy interested in turtles and frogs like me. Dave knew the lay of the land and he knew where the turtles were. Since he was hanging out with my brother, he shared a couple of precious town secrets with me on turtle locations.

He explained why not to even bother with Miller Pond. The turtles generally had an easy escape from being captured, and the city would not allow a kid to be wading around in the pond or setting traps. One could only see the occasional turtle basking in the distance before plunging to safety if threatened.

He clued me in to an unknown pond located behind a junkyard. It was an old gravel pit without a name and it was not known or used by the general public. There was no public parking and it would have to be accessed by bike and then on foot.   Perfect!

If I didn't have turtle-fever before, what happened next launched me into a frenzy. Dave had something to show me. He took me out to his back yard to a shed. He had a key ready and removed the lock. He opened the door, and on the ground near the shed window were two small tubs.

"Have a look" he said. With my mouth open and eyes wide I kneeled down and peered into the containers. One contained a hatchling *Chelydra serpentina* (Common snapping turtle). It was the most amazing thing I had ever seen. I had seen snapping turtles in books and they looked menacing and not really like pet material. This was a baby and it was all black, cute and mesmerizing.

The tub beside the snapping turtle held a *Chrysemys picta bellii (Western painted turtle).* It was not a full-grown adult, and not a hatchling. It was a perfect, small sized turtle with beautiful markings.

Dave picked up the baby snapper and showed me its belly. It still had remnants of the yolk-sac on its tiny plastron so it was a hatchling not long ago. "Wanna' hold it?" he asked easily. "Does he bite?" I asked. "Naaa', go ahead" Delighted, I took the tiny turtle in the palm of my hand. Real life is always better than pictures.

I was pretty young so I must have said something like, "Wow he's so awesome!" but I can only guess. I just remember being amazed. I was also able to hold the painted turtle. I held his shell between the index finger and thumb. He was a nipper so I needed to be careful. Still I was entranced.

I thanked Dave and asked him all the questions I could think of about the turtles, their care and where they came from. He told me more about the secret pond by the dump and then added a new option.

There was a private operation called Walton Pond not far from the same area of the secret pond. Walton Pond was a nature preserve/gravel company that gave access to a few members and paid guests for fishing. The entire area was surrounded by chain-link fencing with a front gate for vehicles. During most days it was just a gravel operation with the ponds unoccupied by any fishermen. Only rarely when passing by in my parents' vehicle did I ever see anyone making use of it.

Dave made his description plainly and with a warning. "There are tons on turtles in that pond but access is for guests only. You could jump the fence, but you'd be trespassing".

"Trespassing", it was an intimidating word. I had heard rumors from other kids about a farmer near our house that would shoot trespassers with rock salt if they were caught trespassing on his property. At my young age, this was what stuck in my mind, not the legal definition or the possibility of being arrested.

I would start with pursuing the low-hanging fruit. The secret pond would give me the first goal to focus on, but I would always have the private lake information stored away in the back of my mind.

My neighbor friend shared my interest in turtles. I told him each and every secret that Dave told me with no concern about the confidence Dave undoubtedly trusted in me. I now had a partner to undertake this journey with.

We made a game plan. Wake up at six a.m., get buckets and pocket knives, ride bikes to secret turtle pond. It was summer and we were free.

The bike ride was mostly uneventful. The wire handle of the bucket simply rested over the handlebar of our bicycles as we rode. Sure it would bounce around wildly, smack into our legs and rub the front tire on sharp turns, but how else does one carry a bucket on a bicycle?

We had a pretty good idea of where the pond was. My old house was a few blocks away from the junkyard that the pond was located behind. After crossing the railroad tracks, we took a path that ran between the tracks and a barbed wire fence.

We made some good progress before the path ran out. Now there was nothing but weeds and railroad tracks. We thought we could try riding our bikes on them but it only took two seconds to understand the ridiculousness of that idea. We would have to park the bikes and hike.

We hid them as best we could near a tree. We had no bike locks with us so we would have to do an extra good job of hiding them. We gathered some weeds and branches and covered the bikes. They were placed on the opposite side of the tree from the path. We were not expecting any thieves to be by, but we took no chances.

We had a barbed wire fence to get through. It was an old fence so creating a gap in the loose wires for each other to crouch down and move through was not difficult. My friend snagged his shirt a bit on the first try, but I was the king of limbo.

We wandered diagonally away from the fence line and in the direction of the junkyard. Having never been to the pond, and knowing it was hidden from view of any road or housing development; we had to hike on faith that we were close and would run into any pond in the area if it was there.

The weeds were thick but we had the energy of a fresh morning and the hope of discovery pushing us through. There was a hill ahead. We weren't too keen on taking the difficult route, but we could see treetops rising from the other side that would hopefully mean some water could be found near their base. Besides, we wanted to stay out of sight as much as possible in the event we were not supposed to be walking in this area.

We walked up the hill and became surrounded by tall weeds, prickly thistles and young cottonwoods. The foliage began to get thick to the point where we had to thrash and meander our way through. We started a descent down the other side and the weeds and brush only got thicker.

The buzzing of flies was becoming noticeable, then came the whining of mosquitos. My friend was starting to complain but I knew we were getting close to the end of the weeds. They were taller than our heads and visibility of what was ahead was nonexistent, but we had to be close.

We were no longer on a steep downward incline and continued to beat a path forward through the foliage. The ground began to soften. I was ten feet ahead of my partner when the weeds broke and I saw water. We had found the pond!

I treaded carefully. I didn't want to storm into the scene like I had just found a pool in the desert. We were at the bottom of a bowl created by an old gravel pit which ended up making a fairly sizable pond. The scene was tranquil, the waters still. Birds were chirping and feasting on insects at the water's surface.

The path opened up to where I could view the length of the pond ahead but there was still a wall of weeds to my right. "We found it!" I said quietly but excitedly. "We did?" my friend returned, still trouncing in the weeds behind me.

I inched forward slowly to get a view of what the pond looked like on the South side around the weeds. A twenty-foot log came into view that was half submerged in the water as it rested on shore, and then I saw them.

Two western painted turtles, one large adult and one juvenile, were basking in the new morning sun at the end of the log. It was one of the most beautiful sights in my memory. It meant that I had found the pond and the turtles of my dreams lived there. I was amazed that taking the chance on a rumor and an unknown area turned out to be successful.

I looked at the scene before me like a beautiful painting. My friend was still behind and I excitedly started waving him to me. "There's turtles here!" I whispered as loud as I could. With one plop and then another, both startled turtles plunged into the water. "There are??" my friend came into the scene sweating and slapping mosquitos. "Where? WHERE?" he asked, frantically. "They were right there!" I pointed. "Look at the ripples!" I hoped.

He looked disappointed. I had to explain what I saw and he had to accept that it was true. We were both happy to have found the pond, however, and went about exploring and looking for turtles. We walked the water's edge where we could, and climbed up higher when we found no shoreline to walk along.

We stopped a bit to rest and look upon our discovery from our now high vantage point. Looking at the water we noticed something. We could see small projections rising from the surface. We would look away, look back, and they would be gone. We got up to look around the pond and saw more of this phenomenon, and then realized that we were looking at turtle heads coming up for air. We could see the outline of the upper carapace below the water if we looked from the right angle. If we startled them with a thrown rock they would drop below the surface for an extended period.

I was glad that my friend was able to get a glimpse of at least part of a turtle that day. I could say that I didn't drag him along on this expedition for nothing. We now had an idea of how turtles behaved and how catching one would not be as easy as simply walking up to it and picking it up. We could only watch them. With no clue on how to catch them, they may as well have been a thousand miles away.

Hot, sweaty and thirsty, we made our way back to our bikes and began the long ride back home with empty buckets. We would have to return another day with another plan.

I felt that we had accomplished a great deal with our new knowledge, but I was now more anxious than ever to have my first wild-caught turtle. We would go back a few times to the pond with no success. It would not be until early spring the following year before we could claim any.

An unseasonably warm April day made us think that spring had arrived. With an unsuccessful summer, and then winter seemingly behind us, we decided to give the pond another try. We arrived not far from our original landing spot where we first encountered the shoreline. We made our way about twenty yards up shore when we saw him.

Up until this point, several visits to the secret pond failed to result in a captured turtle. Now we were looking success dead in the face and it was not what we expected. The face of success was enormous! We were looking down at a huge adult snapping turtle lying lifeless in the mud. In fact we thought him quite dead. But why did he choose to die in such a spot, poised to return to the water?

I had read enough turtle books to know that we had to be careful around these things. We started by looking at him at all angles. There was not a movement, nor a sound. The natural next step would be to find a large stick.

With a little poking we realized that the beast was indeed still alive. He barely poked his nose out from under his shell, but there was life. There was still a chill in the night at this time of year, so we may have caught him coming out, or thinking of coming out, of dormancy.

In my mind this was a success. I had no plan for housing or long term care, but this turtle was coming home with me. I had to think back to what my books said about holding large snapping turtles and soft-shelled turtles. I geared myself up, thought about it a while, planned my angles and went in.

I grabbed the turtle by the back legs and quickly dropped him into our largest bucket. He was still groggy and did not protest much over the whole event. He did stretch his neck out a bit to let out a hiss.

The turtle was so large that he barely fit in our bucket. Fortunately it was industrial sized for the mixing of plaster and gave us a few extra inches. It would be a difficult ride home as the extra weight banged against my thighs. I switched back and forth from the left handlebar to the right. I would stop and rest several times before finally getting home.

We took the bucket to the back yard lawn where we could get a good look at our catch. I pulled the hose out and washed the mud of off his shell to reveal what he truly looked like. There was a quarter inch of moss attached to the shell which would not be coming off with a garden hose. We had a much better sense of how his skin and face looked. He was ugly but awesome.

My mother came out and confirmed his ugliness. "Uhhh! What are you planning on doing with that thing?" she asked disgustedly from the deck above. "Keep it" I responded. "No." She shook her head and dismissed the idea outright. "This is not a little turtle for a pet. We don't have any room for this thing!"

I protested reflexively. I finally found success and couldn't enjoy it. I wanted a turtle so bad, but deep down this was not what I had in mind. Still I defended it. "Can't we build something to keep him in?" I pleaded. "That's way too big. I thought you were talking about a little turtle like this when I said you could have one" She held her hands apart about four inches. "You're gonna' get bit!"

I made one last-ditch effort to make this happen. "But I brought him all the way home on my bike. It's getting late!" "Your sister can drive you back and you can let it go." "Aw-wwww?!" I whined. "She's gonna' take you later. We'll take some pictures of it."

9-inch shell plus body and tail is a decent sized snapper!

For the next few hours we spent time messing with the turtle. It seemed to wake up a bit from the warmth of the sun, but it was still pretty groggy and slow-moving. My mother took a few photos from different angles so at least I would have something to look at later.

My sister came out jingling the car keys. "OK let's get this over with." Obviously my mother had apprised her of the situation while we were messing with the turtle and saying our good-byes to him. My friend decided to go home as we had lost the fight to keep our catch and there was nothing left to say.

I attempted to scoot the turtle back into the bucket but he was now becoming livelier! Time in the sun had given him spunk. He hissed loudly and my sister yelled "Oh my god!" as it surprised her. It surprised me as well, but I was able to corral it into the bucket it as it decided to pick up the pace and crawl in on its own.

Pretty impressive claws, no?

By the time we made it back to the turtle pond it was already dusk. My sister parked the station wagon within a clump of tress, as close as she could to where I told her the path could be found. She walked with me down the path by the railroad tracks. Over the several return trips I had made to the pond, I eventually found the quickest route to the water's edge without having to bust through tall weeds as done on the first visit.

"This place is scary" she said as we made it to the top of the bank. "Just turn it loose and let's get out of here."

I stumbled down the bank with the bucket and made the short hike to the easiest place to access the water. "Mark!" I heard from the distance in a half whisper/half yell. "MARK! Hurry!"

To describe what happened next will mean to offend the sensibilities of many in these modern PC times. But in the town that we lived, the time that we lived in it, and in the circumstances of the evening I can only describe the truth and hope that it paints the moment as experienced.

"The water's cold!" I yelled back. "Mark I hear Mexicans over there! Let's get out of here!" she explained. My sister was around 19 years old at the time, and in this moment she was young and in charge of her pre-teen brother who had little sense of danger.

I took the bucket and upended it to allow the turtle to slide out. He just sat there. I thought it might crawl out to the water when it saw it in front of him, but he just sat there. I decided to try another plan. Maybe he was not ready to come out of dormancy? I realized that it was only April and that we would surely see more snow this year.

"Hold on a second he's going to die if I leave him here" I returned. "Mark we need to get out of here now!" She insisted.

I threw caution to the wind and grabbed the turtle by the base of its large tail where I was previously scared to try earlier in the day. I dragged him over to a large hole by the bank and placed him in there. He made no protest other than a faint hiss. I quickly grabbed clumps of mud at the shore and began throwing it on him.

"What are you doing we need to get the fuck out of here!! I hear them coming!" My sister didn't cuss a lot. I think it may have snapped me out of my concerns for the turtle. "Ok I'm coming!"

By now it was almost dark. I threw the bucket into the weeds in the hopes that I could retrieve it another day. I ran to the bank and started climbing up. My sister was at the top with her hand reaching down as I got close to the top. She grabbed my arm and pulled me up, and at that moment she felt very strong!

"Let's go!" she said. We started walking fast and then I could hear the voices too. I couldn't hear them from the edge of the pond when I was down there. They were laughing and it sounded like a group of them. We couldn't understand them but there was an instinctual interpretation that told us that they were drunken, rowdy men. They were indeed coming closer.

We both walked as fast as we could on the railroad tracks. We glanced behind us but it was too dark to see anything. All we knew is that the voices were growing louder and closer. We wanted to run but the railroad tracks were too tricky to run on. At one point my sister took a fall.

"Shit!" she said. She was very lucky that she didn't break her ankle between the railroad ties. We decided to move to the side of the tracks on the rocks and I would walk ahead of her in a line. The Spanish carousing grew louder.

"Let's run!" she said. I didn't question her and started running. I could hear her behind me and knew that she was there. We ran all the way to the car and could hear that the men were laughing, but their voices quickly grew fainter.

My sister had the keys out and ready before we even reached the car. She was in and reaching over to the passenger side to flip the door lock in a blink of an eye. She started the vehicle as I was climbing in, and as I shut the door we were moving in reverse.

It only took seconds for the station wagon to change from its well-hidden parking space in the trees to barreling into a paved area by the busy road. We were relieved to see the light of a street lamp on a telephone pole, and passing cars that meant safety.

My sister put it in drive and the station wagon was on its way home. She made a brief and passionate explanation of why we had to leave and the rest of the drive home was made in silence. She was clearly freaked out.

We would never know what the intentions were of the men that night. All I know is that my sister was as scared as I'd ever seen her, and I was not one to question it. She had more experience in the ways of the world than I.

I had cried over the loss of a pet before this day. Now I had a different sense of what priority the catching of a turtle or the keeping of any pet fell under, and it was now a little lower than before. As much as I coveted reptiles and amphibians for much of my childhood, teen years and even later, I had an awakening as to how my pursuit of them could have a cost.

All of this made for an interesting day and increased my experience with turtles, but still I was left with no pet turtle, and still I wanted one. After a few more visits to the turtle pond (in the daytime!), I was starting to get desperate. I was willing to try something new.

Walton pond was always in the back of my mind. Working on legend and more rumors from new sources, I returned to thoughts of all the turtles that supposedly could be found there.

Looking at Google Maps decades later in my adulthood, I have to chuckle at how close the two ponds were to each other. At the time, however, Walton pond seemed to be miles further from my house and a much riskier endeavor than even our brush with "danger" at the secret turtle pond.

Desperation will make a person do things that they normally wouldn't. I had a wonderful ten-gallon aquarium sitting empty in my parent's basement. I had set it up with gravel, five inches of water, and a basking area, all for a turtle that wasn't there. I would turn the lamp on and illuminate the tank. I would sit and stare and imagine my turtle swimming inside.

I simply had to know what Walton pond was all about. I was tired of going to the original turtle pond and coming home with nothing. The turtles there had seemingly too much advantage. They could see us stumbling down the bank and had plenty of time to dive down into the safety of the muddy pond bottom. Something different was in order.

We planned our commando mission of Walton pond. Biking to the area, we made a "dry run" inspection of the pond and examined the perimeter fence. We found that the North fence ran along the railroad tracks, the same tracks further down from the original turtle pond. There were plenty of tall weeds running alongside. Ideas were forming.

Two weeks later, we set our alarms on a summer weekday morning for six a.m. We wanted to arrive at Walton pond bright and early, and hopefully before anyone that worked there. We pedaled our bikes, still in darkness, each with one of our trusty buckets in hand.

Arriving at the North fence, everything was quiet. It seemed to me, perfect for our mission. We quickly dismounted in order to keep a low profile. We walked our bikes to the midpoint of the pond behind the fence line and along the ever-familiar railroad tracks. A nice clump of weeds appeared before us, a perfect place to stash bikes.

There was light traffic on the nearby road. We could hear any cars coming from the distance and would be able to time our climb over the chain-link fence so that no passing eyes could witness it.

I would go first. We double-checked the office area for movement, and waited for the silence of the road with no approaching vehicles in sight.

I leaped up and climbed the links as fast as I knew how. I was a good climber and made it to the top quickly. I would have to contend with the barbs of the upper portion of the fence where it ended in nasty, twisted cut-off wires. I was careful to make sure that none of my clothing would get caught, and dropped to the other side. I crouched to the ground as my partner did the same on his side.

We would now pause for a bit to stay hidden and listen. We listened for the expected yell of an adult. It never came. Next, we listened for vehicle traffic. The occasional car passed on the road as normal.

I peeked a bit over the wall of weeds I was crouched in. No one seemed to be coming out of the building or forming a posse. I told my friend that after the next passing car and stretch of road silence, it was his turn.

One final check prompted the signal, followed by "OK now!" in a whisper. My neighbor climbed the fence as fast as he could. He maneuvered over the top and made his way down. "Ow!" he let out as he descended.

We both now hid in the brush and looked things over on him. He had snagged his shirt a bit on the exposed end of the chain-link fence and cut his hand, but it could have been much worse. We now both lay inside the perimeter.

Resting at the top of the bank, we hid among the weeds and peered through. We couldn't see any man or vehicle activity across the pond at the office. There were two cars parked in the parking lot, but that didn't mean anyone was there. It was still quite early.

The pond bank dropped steeply down as our "original" turtle pond did. Both most likely were converted from former gravel pits. The opposite side of the pond was much like ours, covered with weeds in many areas. We may be able to remain unseen from the office once we reached the shoreline at the bottom of the bank.

After studying the chain-link gate entrance and the office area for several minutes, we decided to make the dash to the bottom. We crawled through the brush, stayed low and quickly scooted/slid down the bank. We kept low and maneuvered to an area where we had the tallest weeds blocking our view to the office.

Keeping one eye warry of onlookers, we scanned the pond. Fish were jumping everywhere this calm morning, and we saw ten times the turtle heads peeking up for air than at the other pond. The rumors were true; we were in an excellent spot.

We walked a few yards further along shore while still hidden. From beneath my feet a Western Painted Turtle scrambled from the sand and into the water! For a second I froze, but hesitating would gain me nothing so I went into the water, shoes still on, and gave chase.

The turtle disappeared into some slimy pond weeds and I plunged my hands right into this same area in desperation. I thought I had lost yet another turtle and then felt the shape of its shell within the handful of weeds in my grasp. I pulled the clump from the water, unraveled the weeds, and revealed a nipping and angry little turtle, a perfect juvenile of only four inches!

I came to shore and removed the remaining slime from his shell. Was he ever beautiful! My friend and I were shocked and excited, but now we were suddenly paranoid. We were in no way authorized to be here, yet found what we wanted in a short amount of time. Instead of pushing our luck we chose to just get in and get out.

Scrambling up the bank, we were less careful about being seen, but remained crouched as we moved. I held the turtle in one hand and climbed with the other. He mostly had his head tucked into his shell at this point.

At the fence line we decided that my friend would go first. "Hurry, but be careful this time!" I didn't want either of us to get snagged again. He made it up and over without a hitch. Now we would do some creative juggling. With both hands, I lowered the turtle for momentum. "Ready?" I said. My friend looked excited, apprehensive and amused all at once. "Oh my god... OK ready!"

I "gently" launched the turtle into the air. It cleared the top of the fence and my friend danced frantically with his hands held up. He made a glorious catch.

Once I saw that the turtle had made it to the other side unhurt, I started climbing. I was up and over in record time, but now it was my turn to get my clothing snagged. I heard the rip and felt the tear in my skin as my shirt caught the sharp wire when I dropped to the ground. It was then that I heard the "Hey! Hey!!" coming from the building across the pond. We didn't bother to even look toward the direction of the sound; we placed the turtle into the bucket, mounted our bicycles and sped as fast as we could pedal in the opposite direction.

I heard some unintelligible yelling behind me but we kept riding - and laughing! It was a combination of exhilaration, fear and two trouble-making kids thinking they knew it all.

Looking back on it, this was by far the best turtle I had ever caught. It was perfect in size, and at that juvenile stage it still had its striking markings and had not yet begun to grow algae on its shell. It graced my aquarium for years after.

We never did return to Walton pond. I guess we felt that we had dodged a bullet, and also that our mission was accomplished. Besides, in our minds we were wanted criminals by the men that worked there, and it would be wise to never return.

We would return to the original turtle pond on many occasions. Over the years I caught a baby version of the snapping turtle we had originally caught there. I learned to make turtle traps and tested them there with good success in catching more painted turtles.

The original pond is gone now, but the city has since created a network of ponds and paths in its place after purchasing the land. The area is now a public park giving kids a legal, albeit less adventurous, outlet for the chasing of critters.

Part II

Road Lizard

Like a switch, one day my interest in turtles was shut off and I became obsessed with lizards. I must have come across a library book about lizards or South American wildlife one day. Probably a coffee table book with large glossy photos of animals made by world-famous photographers.

I was a sucker for these books, and they would send me off on my obsessions. I would now find each and every book possible that focused on lizards, and scour them over and over.

My first captive lizards were the unsurprising and commonly available *Anolis carolinensis* (Green anole) found in pet stores. They were referred to as "chameleons" in the pet stores at that time. In my case, a classmate heard of my interest in lizards and turned over two unwanted pets from his home to mine, including a ten-gallon aquarium!

Despite my elation upon getting them home and marveling at their brilliant green hue on the first day, the green quickly went away. I applied everything I knew to setting up the perfect enclosure and taking care of these animals, but what I knew had large gaps in details of their proper care.

The lizards survived my care for maybe half a year. I could never know for sure if it was a heavy diet of meal worms or the excessive humidity of my setup, but one of the few times that I saw the lizards green again was when I found them dead in the cage. An utter failure for my first attempt, and it would not be my last.

I decided to get serious about my lizard keeping skills. I eventually saved up enough money to buy a specimen that I had my eye on at the local pet store. Still of the "anolis" world, the store had a solitary *Anolis sagrei* (Brown anole) that I had to have.

I loved how muscular and tough he looked even though he was not as pretty as my green anoles. He was tiny, but looked like a mean little bully with the expression he held and a "bring it on" look. I named him Thor.

I redoubled my efforts to improve my skills in lizard keeping so as not to make the same mistakes made with the first pair of anoles. I read and re-read every book I had at home, and every book the library offered on lizards as pets.

I was able to provide a nice variety of insect foods that I caught in the yard and in the house. This would be supplemented by trips to the pet store and purchasing crickets, as opposed to the meal worms I used before.

I made sure that the aquarium was properly ventilated with a fitted screen so that my specimen was not subjected to constant humidity and mold. I diligently sprayed the tank at daily intervals to provide water, since the way anoles normally drink is from droplets, rather than a water bowl.

Things were going quite well. I was adding to the terrarium with unique rocks and branches that I came across. I gradually had it set up just the way I wanted it. I took time out of each day to sit and watch the terrarium in the dark, with only the cage light illuminating the room. As a young man, it was like gazing at a Christmas tree.

Fall would arrive early that year. Insects were getting more difficult to find. Whereas before I could stroll around the lawn and flower beds to pick up grasshoppers, worms and crickets at my leisure, now I was spending half an hour or longer just to find one stray insect.

My mother would help out when she could to bring me to the pet store and buy crickets. These would be purchased in quantities of twenty or so, and I would attempt to keep them alive as long as possible for daily feedings. Most would die off eventually, as cricket keeping information was sparsely available at the time.

There came a period of time when I would not be able to get a ride to the pet store any time in the near future. I had used up all of my live crickets, so decided to look outside for something to tide Thor over. It was cool out. I was searching all of my usual spots in the flower beds for something, anything that was crawling around in the insect world. There was nothing.

I took a break under the porch to think a bit when I saw something out of the corner of my eye, crawling on the concrete slab that I was standing on. It was a black, beetle-like creature. Hell, it wasn't beetle-like it was a beetle! I sprang into action and scooped it up in my hands. This was the beginning of a huge mistake.

I kept the beetle sealed in my cupped hand as I made my way back inside. I could feel it running around in the dark "cage" I had created as it searched for a way out. I always felt a little nervous doing this with any insect, expecting a little bite or pinch in defense, but of course that never came. I opened the screen if the aquarium lid and tossed him in.

Thor jumped off the branch he was perched upon. He easily overcame the beetle and took it into his mouth. After one or two openings and closings of the mouth he swallowed the critter whole.

I felt pretty good about myself, having provided nourishment for my pet in lean times. I moved on to other endeavors for my day.

The next day was a Monday and a long school day. All I wanted to do was watch my after school shows, have a snack and relax. After my shows and some couch time I decided to wander to the basement where my aquarium and Thor resided. I pressed the switch of the overhead lamp and revealed the scene of horror.

Thor was perched on his branch, I was ready to relax and observe him but something did not look right, His head was drooped and resting on the branch in a manner uncharacteristic if a reptile. Only a mammal would allow gravity to take over and the neck to go limp like this during sleep.

I was uncertain as to what was going on. I just knew that he didn't look right. I then noticed the beetle scurrying around in the corner of the tank. What the hell was going on here?

I removed the lid and looked down over the top of Thor to get a look at him from another angle. A rush of realization overtook me when I saw the hole in his side. It was all over, Thor was gone. The armored beetle had simply bored his way out.

I was infuriated! Before I took any action I made one last attempt at hope and picked Thor up from his perch. Of course he was lifeless. It was my ignorance that Thor paid dearly for, but I would take my revenge and shame out on that god damn beetle just the same.

In a rage I went upstairs and grabbed a cigarette lighter from the kitchen drawer. I ran back down to the cage, found the beetle and grabbed him. I took him outside under the deck, set him on the concrete and went at him with the lighter. I took my time and took twisted satisfaction in the creature's reaction to his predicament

After getting the lighter treatment out of my system, I took a rock to what was left of the pathetic remains of his body. Each pound was accompanied by thoughts of Thor and anger at myself, until the beetle was nothing but a slightly moist, gravelly substance that could be dashed over a salad.

My finest hour? Probably not. Knowing the future might have taken the edge off a bit. At my current home near the Gulf of Mexico, my dog spends the entire day chasing this same species of lizard. I can observe dozens of them by simply walking out my back door and having a seat.

The highly invasive brown anole found all over my future house.

Once an exotic species from Cuba, they have spread all over the Caribbean and U.S. gulf states by hitching a ride on boats and other vehicles. They are even pushing out the native green anole in many areas.

It hurt at the time though. It would be years before I got back on the horse of insectivorous lizard keeping.

Part III

Frogphibians

I turned my attention to the local frog and toad population. Having only been exposed to leopard frogs at our cabin thus far, I was getting curious about new and different species. I did not have the experience of seeing or catching any different anurans until our family moved to another part of town.

This new home development was situated along a golf course with multiple water hazards in addition to an irrigation creek running behind some of the houses. I wasn't keen on moving from our old home until I realized the amount of new critters in the area that I could enjoy.

One of the new neighborhood kids, we'll call him Dave, had some information on a frog and toad paradise that was a half hour bike ride away. According to Dave, we would be dealing with the possibility of encounters with angry farmers armed with shotguns full of rock-salt. I was starting to wonder if this was all just a scary story that people told.

The venture somehow grew into an entire team of boys gathering their bikes and buckets. This would be the largest contingency of herp hunters that I have been a part of with the six members that caught word of, and took interest in the excursion. Of note now that I am much older and interested in such observations, is that none of us owned, could access, could afford, anything resembling a net.

That would certainly not stop us as we ambled down a surprisingly busy road to reach our hunting grounds. It was windy that day, and between that and my large bucket on the handle bars, I would swerve on occasion to compensate.

At one point there was a large gust that shoved me toward the shoulder of the road. This occurred on a bit of a turn and I countered the wind and found myself too far into the road. At the same time a truck honked and I looked up to see a large, angry man in a truck shaking his fist as he passed. Sorry!

We peddled until we reached the bridge that passed over the St. Vrain River. Once our bikes were hidden from view on the sloping banks, we had to contend with the ubiquitous barbed wire that would forever attempt to keep us out from such places. After a few careful trots down the bank, the hunt was on.

Walking along the river's shore, I could tell that it would be a new and interesting spot for critters. Minnows darted in and out of visibility. Bird life was abundant. There were smaller streams that diverted into still pools with watercress and cattails. It just felt froggy.

It would not be the pools that held our attention at first; however, a sand bar seemed to be coming alive as we approached it. Toads, dozens and dozens of them! *Bufo boreas* (now *Anaxyrus boreas*) is the Western Toad, and we had stumbled upon a bumper crop of toadlets that were wondering where to begin their lives.

We set our buckets down and the collection began. No special skills were required, simply chase them down and scoop them up with your hands and place them into the waiting open bucket. There was no thought given to the amounts collected, population impact, or proper permitting, it was simply – Toads! Get em'!

What an exciting moment for all of us, but particularly for me. I had never even seen a toad before, and now I was seeing scores of them and able to grab as many as I wanted. I couldn't believe that after all of the days coming home with nothing after an animal hunt, there could be so many available at once.

Bliss was interrupted by our guide. "Wait! Get come here! Get down!!" Dave yelled and whispered at the same time. We all heard him and followed as he waved us in and crouched-walked to the bank.

"What's wrong?" I asked. "That farmer" he whispered, "He doesn't want people around here and he's outside." We peered over the bank just enough to see the cowboy hat of a man walking along his property. We waited and were glad to see that he only spent a few minutes in view before getting into his truck and driving off, presumably into town.

With this minor distraction behind us, we were back to collecting. Each of us took as many toads as we wanted, without much thought of why or where to house them, there was just an impulse to collect that we all shared.

With the toad harvest completed, we put our buckets down in order to explore the area without being dragged down by the load. There was a lot of nice habitat to be seen in a relatively small area. A baby trout would be sighted here, a garter snake there, and jumping *Lithobates catesbeianus* (American bullfrogs) too!

I had never seen a wild bullfrog in my life. There was obviously a separation of preferred habitat between bullfrogs in the lower foothills elevation and the leopard frogs just forty minutes away in the mountains. I was definitely excited about encountering these, as they were larger frogs decked out in a beautiful green skin.

We only caught one bullfrog that day with our entire group trying, but I definitely planned to be back to try again. We finally made our way back to the closest house that one of us lived, parked our bikes, and gathered our buckets. We began the process of taking inventory.

There was such excitement as we greedily and carelessly dumped our buckets onto the driveway to enjoy our bounty. We counted over fifty toads in addition to the one bullfrog.

We selected a few of our favorites, made trades, and after all the excitement, let quite a few go into the nearby irrigation ditch. I did try to trade all of my toadlets for the one bullfrog, but no go. Still, I was happy with my bucket of success.

I brought home my catch of ten toadlets and searched for a container to house them. I had since acquired another turtle so my ten-gallon aquarium was occupied. I was able to convince my mother to allow me the use of a large glass container which could have passed as a jumbo fishbowl, but was a bit too decorative for such a purpose.

I filled the bowl halfway with sand, inserted a small water pool, and decorated it with stones and bark. I placed my catch into their new habitat and began a fascination with frogs and toads in captivity.

I would make regular trips back to the lower St. Vrain River for frog hunts. I became adept at catching the bullfrogs that seemed so elusive back at my first outing. It's amazing what the proper tool for the job can do. In addition to bullfrogs, I was lucky enough to encounter and catch a solitary *Pseudacris triseriata* (Western chorus frog). I was surprised that something so close to the exotic tree frogs seen in my books could be found so close to home!

It was nice to have such a long stretch of good luck in the trespassing department before it slowly began to run out. I suppose a ten-year-old can get away with much more than a teenager. When a local farmer finally flashed his shotgun and yelled at me during a lone trip to the river, it was finally time to seek new hunting grounds.

I quickly switched from one trespassing violation to another via the city golf course. At the very least, there would likely not be gunplay to contend with here.

Alone or with my neighbor, I would jump the ditch that acted as the border to the course. We then would assess if the coast was clear as best as we could, then make a mad dash across the fairway to the water traps. Here we could find at least some small amount of cover in the form of tall grass and cattails.

At these ponds we could occasionally see turtles, but mostly there were bullfrogs, and plenty of them! On one particular bumper-crop day we were able to fill our buckets with the biggest tadpoles I had ever seen. We must have visited the pond late in the spring as they were in varying stages of development, from no legs at all, to four limbs popping out and fully functional. All were large, chunky and brilliant green in color.

As we completed our trip and began to pack up I noticed a golf cart, a GREEN golf cart. We had learned over the years that green golf carts were unique in that anyone driving a green golf cart was a staff member of the golf course. Golfers would usually play in white golf carts, sometimes red or blue, but never green! Also, staff golf carts were gas-driven, not electric. This meant that they travelled fast as far as golf carts go.

I alerted our friend to the coming danger. Coming toward us "fast" was a green golf cart with a "man" in it. At the time, anyone in their late teens was a man to us, and a scary proposition. We had rebellion in us, however, and the need for herping was more powerful than the fear of any man that could chew us out, catch us, or call our parents if they recognized us.

We were pretty fast kids. Most kids can be when they want to. We ran to the most logical place to escape danger, which may seem counter-intuitive at first. It was the route directly in the path that the golf cart was heading. All we had to do was get across the fairway to the irrigation ditch that ran beside it.

With our buckets of tadpoles sloshing about and banging against our thighs, we ran. We ran with fear and with determination. We were confident that we would make it in time. We came to the edge of the fairway and arrived at the ditch.

Normally we would take care to find a narrow part of the ditch to leap across in order to save our sneakers from soaking. There would be no such concerns now as we needed to cross the ditch with no time to spare. We simply jumped in and ran across, our shoes sloshing and our pants soaking to our knees.

Once across we slowed to a casual jog and then a brisk walk. The cart arrived at the other side of the bank seconds after we crossed. The young man driving began barking at us. "Hey!" We didn't turn our heads. "HEY!!" he tried again. We kept walking. "I know where you live!" he attempted. We both laughed at this and picked up the pace. Just in case he was right, we decided to change direction and walk the wrong way for a while.

After taking the long way home, any fear of reprisals from the course marshal vanished as we sorted our take. My neighbor happened to have an unused baby swimming pool that would be perfect for this. We filled it half way up with water, dumped the contents of our buckets in, and watched the fun.

Huge tadpoles made their way around the pool in their slow and steady pace. Green heads being propelled by a wiggling tail. We noted the elite few of head-starters that were already in the latter part of metamorphosis. These would have to be divvied up between us and any other kids around that may want one.

The majority would be released into the ditch that ran behind our back yards on the opposite side of the eighteen-hole golf course we had just trespassed upon. Never before did we encounter even a single bullfrog when searching this ditch, but that would soon change.

That ditch ended up being a thriving home for countless bullfrogs upon completion of their metamorphosis. So much so, that I would witness an ugly side of this abundance.

Due to our overstocking efforts, we had become accustomed to seeing and hearing plentiful plops in the water in the ditch behind our houses. What was once a hot commodity could now be easily acquired with little effort. We had kept specimens we like in our home aquariums and observed them until we got bored of them, at which time we simply let them go into the ditch.

Then, the Fourth of July season came around. This meant the annual pilgrimage to Wyoming as most of the good fireworks were illegal in our state. After one such fireworks run, we were laden with firecrackers and bottle rockets in addition to frogs, and life was good.

One day my neighbor came and invited me to witness something. It seems that they had become bored with blowing up tin cans and now had selected a bullfrog to vaporize with a Thunderbomb. I was appalled.

I am not much of an activist but this kind of act simply didn't sit well with me. I loved my friends and we had great times together but this was not something I was down with. Nevertheless, I pretended to be interested.

At first I tried to talk them out of the idea. They argued that there were hundreds of frogs out back, so I knew that they would be going through with it. I asked if I could hold the frog and have a look at it. They reluctantly obliged and probably had a feeling for what I would do next, but they allowed it anyway.

As soon as I had the frog in my hands I took off running. I was the fastest of the group, in addition to being able to jump fences with ease. I made it over their yard's fence and down the creek path in a flash, and kept going as they attempted to keep up. I looked ahead as I ran in order to find a portion of the creek of suitable width.

The creek was full this time of year and I saw the target I was looking for. Once upon it I tossed the frog forward and he plunged into the water. I saw a couple of firm pumps of the rear legs and he was lost in the depths. I left my friends yelling "We knew you would do that!" and as angry with me as I was with them.

Sometimes kids have disagreements and this was one we put behind us not long after.

The passing years of my early teens would be filled with field adventures of all types. My ten gallon aquarium and others that I acquired later would house many different species, some local and some inexpensive pet store finds.

Off of memory I can recall box turtles, snapping turtles, chorus frogs, newts, salamanders - anything that I could get my hands on and experience. Some would be let go, some would die, and others would be traded. Notably absent during this time were snakes, as this was a house guest that my mother would not tolerate.

My high school years were a bit of an off time for reptiles and amphibians in my life. I would still have something in my aquarium at any given time, but there was much less field work going on. We were becoming young men, and socializing with girls was dominating our interest much more than other creatures. Jobs and spending money took over our summertime outdoor ventures.

Part IV

Freedom to Fail

During my college years I had a resurgence of herp interest. Not so much in field work, more in captive specimens. Maybe it was helped by living away from home and being able to keep anything I wanted. I also had a little more money to spend and a vehicle to get around to any pet store around the state that interested me.

On one particular visit to see friends in Denver, I was compelled to visit the local pet shop near their house. Besides the obvious improvement in selection compared to my home town pet shops, there was one particular animal that instantly caught my eye.

In a darkly lit area of the shop that was made to look like a cave or grotto, there was a series of tanks nicely set up with plants and aquatic features. There were turtles for sale, water dragons, fire-bellied toads, newts. This shop was much more inviting and exciting than others I had seen.

At the far end of the reptile room, second row from the floor, sat the tank that caught my eye. A hatchling *Caiman crocodilus* (Spectacled Caiman) sat proudly on his log above a trickling artificial waterfall. His giant, baby crocodilian eyes had me entranced. His skin was glistening and highlighted with distinct, con-trasted markings.

I took my eye off him only long enough to check around the cage setup for a price tag. Fifty dollars!

Fifty dollars was certainly not a small amount of money for me during this time. I needed every spare dollar I could find. But compared to prices I had seen in mail-order catalogs, over two hundred dollars in most cases, this was a bargain.

This was back in the days where most estab-lishments accepted checks. I happened to have my checkbook in my vehicle. I didn't give it any more thought than drinking a glass of wa-ter, and the purchase was made. My friend, not in to reptiles, was with me at the time and thought I was insane.

I was in Denver for a weekend of partying. I had forgotten all about that as I watched the nice shop worker carefully package the little guy in a box with a plastic lining and a moist towel. I found it hard to believe that I was tell-ing my friend that I would be heading back to my apartment at the university sixty miles north, and he was incredulous.

For once I had the presence of mind to skip the partying for another weekend. This was not a common occurrence, because at that time of life I never missed out on a party and the fun involved therein. I looked forward to each one as if there would never be another. It took a caiman to distract me this time.

I needed to get my new acquisition to its new home. I wasn't even completely certain what this new home would be, but I did have three aquariums to work with at my apartment. The one I had in mind, however, was not empty. There would be some rearranging to do.

I had two piranhas at the time in my ten-gallon aquarium. Yes, my taste for critters was not entirely within the herp world. I liked anything exotic. I would have had a monkey given the chance.

As I drove home I had plenty of time to give it some thought. I could move the piranhas into a homemade, five-gallon aquarium that I made out of glass panes and silicone caulk. I would then have the ten-gallon tank freed up for the caiman.

I pulled over three times during my journey back in order to check on its well-being. He was fine of course, but still I checked. His big yellow eyes just stared and I could see his throat moving, a sure sign of breathing and that all was well.

Once home I rushed to get everything done. The poor piranhas were treated like yesterday's news as I dumped them into their smaller quarters. I stole the artificial plants from their home as well.

I went down to the common area of the apartment complex where I was able to collect plenty of good-sized stones from the land-scaping. From a neighboring house, I slipped away with a small log from their firewood pile.

I have to admit, I was able to put together a nice looking semi-aquatic habitat with what I scraped together. The tank was filled about one quarter with water. The log fit nicely across the width of the tank and sat in the middle. Rocks behind it created a backdrop land area and the plants made it all quite believable to the eye.

Now to add the specimen. I had never han-dled a crocodilian of any kind so I wasn't sure what to expect. I opened the box and there he was again, eyeing me. I darted my hand in and grabbed him behind the neck, he opened his mouth in protest in an attempt to nip me, an instinct that ultimately, he would never lose.

The only thing that mattered now was his new home. I gently lowered him into the water area of the tank and released. He seemed un-affected as he gently propelled himself with two easy wags of his tail to the log and crawled up on it.

It was time for the topper. I shut of all of the lights in my room and hit the aquarium hood lamp. I propped myself up on the bed for maximum comfort and just took in the scene. Aquariums lit up in a dark room always gave me an amazing feeling no matter what was in it. Today I was in heaven.

He seemed very comfortable with his new home. He explored a bit, but not in a way that seemed frantic or desperate to get out. I relaxed and watched him for hours in awe of how he moved, how his eyes sparkled and how his markings boldly stood out against the back-drop, even as they blended in.

I fell asleep to the calming scene in my bed-room and got a good night's sleep. The next day I knew that this animal would need some-thing to eat. I got myself ready and made the trip to the local pet shop and purchased five feeder goldfish. This ended up being the perfect first offering.

I added two goldfish to the tank and kept the remaining in a holding container that I found among my limited housewares. The caiman didn't waste much time and took after them. I looked away thinking he would need a few tries, and looked back to see an orange tail flopping from his mouth. Verifying that I had a good eater, it was time to name him.

I had been in a phase of watching a lot of Italian mob movies. I wanted a tough sounding name that could be reminiscent of such things. I decided to name "him" Rocco. I say "him" in quotes, because I would have Rocco for the next ten years and never had him sexed.

That certainly did not make a difference. Over the years Rocco would always be known as a male. He began growing and putting on weight immediately, which is where the fun really started.

In three years he would triple in size. By this time I was in a new rental house and had purchased a new thirty-gallon aquarium for him. A rental house during college years meant only one thing - lots of parties!

My first mishap with Rocco took place during one such party. Yes indeed there was drinking involved that evening and the subject of Rocco came up. Friends wanted to know how I pick him up.

I demonstrated this technique the same way that I always did, and as always Rocco had his mouth gaping open as I held him, but never reaching to bite me. This is when the question was posed "Has he ever bitten you?" I responded that he hadn't. "How bad would it be if he bit you?" Feeling curious and feeling other ways, I replied "Well, let's see."

I wish I could properly explain myself here. All I can say is that curiosity got the best of me, and a little pain was not always a deterrent for me. I placed my finger DIRECTLY into Rocco's mouth and waited, and I didn't have to wait long. For a few seconds Rocco did nothing, and then he chomped.

Still a young caiman, Rocco had needle-like teeth at this time. I came very close to having the top of my finger severed. There was plenty of blood and plenty of laughter. After patching myself up, I moved on to other things that night, but I now understood that Rocco could bite and do real damage.

He would continue to grow and as I moved into new houses with new roommates, Rocco would be along for the ride. He would often be the life of the party and certainly a conversation piece for our guests.

At a certain point Rocco would need a larger enclosure. I was upgrading his living quarters every two years. At the last house of my college years it was just me and one other roommate. I had crafted a large wooden enclosure with a pond and a glass front, using the cheapest glass I could find.

As before, we were hosting parties fairly often. I was at a point now, however, that I thought it would be best to keep Rocco in my room and away from other curious hands. This worked for the most part.

People would ask about Rocco and I would provide viewings in my room, but I would be sure to escort them out and back to the party. As parties go, however, people will wander. At one particular soirée, I was enjoying myself in the living room where I expected everyone to be, when I heard a bit of a ruckus.

People were yelling and the faint sound of a screech came from my bedroom! I rushed in to find a young lady standing in front of Rocco's cage, seemingly in a state of shock. The glass that made the front wall of the enclosure was shattered. Rocco was in the corner and looked at us warily in a frozen pose.

I checked on the girl. She was a little freaked out and didn't know what to say but she looked unharmed. Rocco had been known to whip his tail when he felt threatened and this happened unintentionally from time to time. I didn't ask her what she did because I wanted no kind of trouble this evening. I simply surmised that she had probably messed with him a bit; he flipped out and thrashed his tail, which shattered the front glass.

My thinking was that it was me that used the cheapo glass and exposed myself to the possibility of an accident. I reassured her that it wasn't her fault and suggested that she return to the party and that everything would be OK. I missed a good chunk of the party because of this chick, but I had only myself to blame and started my cleanup task. I believe she ended up leaving. It all could have been much worse.

Rocco and his new farm trough. I can't recall where I stole such a cool rock from?

There would be no more homemade enclo-sures for me for a while. With school getting more intense and my tools and materials lim-ited, I went with an easy fix. I went down to the local farm supply store and purchased a small plastic watering trough for goats and horses. Small in the watering trough world made for a pretty large and deep tub for a young croco-dilian.

I still had more herp diversions at this time. The opportunities just continued to present themselves. During my last year of college, my roommate Dave and I decided to do a proper spring break trip. We settled on Mazatlán Mexico.

On arrival we were propelled straight into the local fun. There was drunken horseback riding on the beach. There were drunken wet T-shirt contests. There were drunken pool par-ties, and there were drunken excursions into town for restaurants and shopping.

At the first visit into town, I was greeted by teenage boys carrying *Iguana iguana* (Green iguanas) of all sizes. Medium sized iguanas were only five bucks! Wow, this place had everything.

Both Dave and I were easily sold on them and we decided that our hotel room needed some mascots. We each purchased two of roughly two feet in length. I doubt we paid more that fifteen dollars for the four.

We kept the fellas in the bathroom of the hotel. Lady guests of ours would let out a screech upon use of the toilet, which would leave us howling in laughter. We probably gave each of them names (the iguanas) but who in the hell remembers?

After a week of debauchery it was time to make our way back to the states, but what to do with these guys? We decided it would be wrong to leave any man behind.

I had brought along with me one pair of extremely baggy pants. In fact, this was the time of "parachute pants". A very long time ago indeed, but this fashion statement provided the perfect solution for storing live luggage.

With everything packed I prepared the team for transportation. I had a pair of long shorts on and put the cargo pants on over them. The long claws of the wild-caught iguanas would cling to the front of the shorts and their presence would be masked by the extra baggy pants. My buddy had his own method for his which I do not recall.

The plane trip back would be similar to the one arriving. Lots of drinking and rowdiness due to the entire plane being occupied by college spring breakers. A very different time indeed for air travel.

During the flight, I transferred my specimens from the pants setup into a carry-on backpack. Many on the flight were aware of this and no one had the thought or inclination to make an issue of it. It was all part of the fun. Upon arriving in the US, it was time to prepare them once again for pantsportation.

We filed out of the plane and made our way to customs. I was now having second and third thoughts about the entire plan, but these were all too late. We had been joking about how to respond if they asked if I had an iguana in my pants. I would reply with "Thank you!" and continue on my way.

None of that seemed very funny upon the sight of customs officials. At the time though, we were not greatly concerned. There was no big international push as there is today to stop illegal wildlife transport. There were certainly laws, and we were hiding them for a reason, but drugs were the primary concern of customs at that time.

I am very happy to say that both of us passed through customs effortlessly. Dave was even a heavy pot smoker and I doubt he did any kind of laundry before he packed for home. To the authorities we probably just looked as we were, like drunken college idiots coming back from spring break.

This would not be my only smuggling operation, but only one or two come to mind for my lifetime. I was not so committed to the craft and was never much for taking great risks with the law. I valued my freedom too much.

I did have occasion to bump up against one herp guru that was devoted to such things. At the time of my senior year in college he was the largest reptile dealer out of Florida. There is no need to refer to him by name, but people in the herp world know to whom I am referring. He famously would pay the price for taking certain risks and was in an entirely different league than I with my silly spring break caper.

This dealer did have a truly amazing inventory, however. I would receive his catalogs and dream of having the money to make certain purchases. Everything I had ever wished for was available. Rhinoceros iguanas, dwarf crocodiles, albino sliders, some items commanded top prices, others were amazing bargains.

I decided to make an attempt at making some extra money to fund my future move to

California. I made a small investment with this outfit that would provide me with a box of *Python regius* (Ball Pythons) for the same price as *one* available in any pet store in my area.

Ball pythons were nowhere near as popular thirty years ago as they are now. These days they are the go-to python due to their manageable size and colorful morphs developed over the years. Back then, everyone wanted *Boa constrictor constrictor* (Red-tailed Boas) or *Python bivittatus* (Burmese Pythons). I took a chance that I could turn a profit on these.

I remember driving an hour and a half to pick up my delivery from the Denver International Airport. My first animal freight pickup! For some reason this seemed awesome to me.

It was literally a wooden crate that said "Live Animals" on it, just like I had seen in the movies. I even used a pry bar to open it up Bugs Bunny style. What an exciting thing for a young man fascinated with such things.

Within the crate there were ten cloth containers. Basically small pillow cases. Each had a hefty lump of snake that could be felt inside, with a knot tied to keep it secure.

I had almost no experience with snakes at this point. I had certainly never worked with constrictors. I was cautious and uncertain, but there was only one way to learn but to dive in and get started. The unpacking would have to begin.

I untied the knot of the first case and turned it upside down. It was alive, a good sign and it looked quite healthy. I didn't handle it much. It was taking on the classic ball position of the ball python, so I simply picked up the ball and transferred it to the aquarium I had prepared for them.

Looking at the rest of the cases, they all sat waiting in the compressed ball state for unpacking. The pace picked up a bit as I unpacked more. The third one caught me off guard however. I was looking at the state of the specimens I had already placed in the aquarium and thus turned my head. For a second, out of the corner of my eye, I thought the one I was currently working with struck out, but I wasn't certain because there was only a quick flash of movement. I kept at my work and placed him in the cage without incident.

I began to notice something else as well. There were things attached to these snakes. At first I thought they were tagged or had unusual scales. After pulling on one I had the realization that these were all wild-caught specimens from Africa.

I spent the rest of the day cautiously going through snake by snake and removing the ticks. Considering they were wild-caught specimens, they were quite tolerant of this large being that was pulling and prodding on them, all but one.

I was saving the handling of the biggest snake for last, the same one that may have struck out earlier. I even managed to remove a couple of his tics without picking him up. At a certain point however, I had to, and I had a bad feeling about it.

I had to get at one the tics attached in an awkward position. He didn't waste much time in chomping down on my hand.

The bite of boas and pythons, it turns out, are no joke when the snake means business. There is no strike-and-release as with some snakes, this one chomped and held. They are blessed with row after row of small but very sharp teeth for gripping, and the grip was succeeding nicely.

I ended up having to slowly pry this monster's mouth off of my hand. Each one of his sharp little teeth got in a good scrape on their way out like a rasp. I bled a bit and disinfected myself with whatever a college student has on hand, and took a break for the time being.

All ten snakes ended up being completely de-ticked. I placed ads in the Denver and local newspapers and announced to everyone I knew that I had pythons for sale.

One by one I sold each python. It was nice having them around as I waited for interested parties to respond. These were the days before mobile phones internet ads, so it was necessary to meet people in person arranged via land-line calls. It is amazing looking back on it that they were all sold within a couple of months, but this was the only way of operating at the time, and it worked.

Once again, all of this was carried out in order to fund my move to Southern California. I wanted to work on the west coast and experience another part of the country. I packed as much as I could, including Rocco in his big tub, into the back of my old Mitsubishi pickup truck, and off I went.

I was taking a scenic route in order to visit a girl I had been seeing from Oregon that moved back home. This meant that I would be traveling through Wyoming and Wyoming weather.

During this stretch of the trip things were getting pretty cold outside. The windswept highways during the fall months are well known to people in that part of the country, but

I had forgotten this. As I happily traveled down the road with my heater on, it hit me that Rocco may not be enjoying it in the back of the shelled pickup.

I found a safe place to pull over in God knows where. I was not in a hurry, and could take minor roads and highways to enjoy the scenery. It was freezing outside and windy. A layer of ice was building up on the outside of the vehicle.

I popped open the camper shell, moved aside the makeshift lid over Rocco's tub and peered inside. He was still and lifeless. I prodded him with one of the long tools I had in the back, no movement. I've killed him!

I reached in and picked Rocco up, he sagged over lifelessly. I had several cardboard boxes in the back that were packed with my things. I found one of significant size and dumped its contents of books out into the truck bed. I quickly stuffed him into the box and tucked all four lids into each other to make a seal, and brought the box into the cab with me.

The truck was still running. I turned the heat up to full and placed the box behind the passenger side of the bench seat. I continued the drive with the heat cranked, going mile after mile and not wanting to believe what had happened. Poor, poor Rocco, what had I done?

The time came to refill the gas tank and get some snacks. This was probably two hours after the discovery of his lifeless body. After filling up and coming back from the convenience store, I decided to give the box a check.

I reached into the back of the cab area and touched the box, nothing. I began to undo the tucked in cardboard lids and BOOM, SCRATCH, BOOM went Rocco's powerful tail and scraping claws against the side of the box. He had been reheated, and was now back from the dead.

Life with Rocco would be uneventful for a couple of years. After finding my first job relating to my degree, I got rid of the tub in exchange for a more visually appealing, sixty-gallon aquarium.

I experienced my first earthquake at the second apartment I rented in San Diego. I sensed some odd movement in the building but couldn't quite make out what it was. Standing near Rocco's tank, I watched him swaying as the water around him made waves back and forth. This was the extent of the earthquake as experienced at this distance from the epicenter.

It turned out to be aftershocks from a significant quake in the LA area.

In yet another home that I briefly rented with four other guys, two moved out. This left us remaining renters unable to continue the expensive lease. I moved everything into the new apartment that we were forced to switch to, everything except Rocco and his aquarium, which I planned to save for the very last. My roommate received a phone call from a panicked and angry former landlord inspecting the moving progress, explaining that there was a three-foot alligator in one of the bedrooms.

Five years of switching apartments and roommates took its toll, so I decided to get my own place with Rocco as my sole roommate from now on. This was the best move I had made as I could enjoy my entire apartment to myself and not worry about whose life situation may change things around yet again. Much of my reptile and amphibian hobby took a pause at this time.

There were two significant adventures that I arranged, however, that were devoted to some exotic herping. These were trips for which I saved up money and vacation time for two years in a row. Each would last eight to ten days, and both were in Central America.

The first trip I took was to Costa Rica. This was at a time when few people were visiting Central America, before a lot of the tourism infrastructure was set up and only a few Americans were beginning to travel there.

It was an amazing trip. I set out to join two old school friends at the beginning. We slept at the base of an active volcano and had some great party days at the beach. I then decided to go it alone and pursue other adventures for the rest of the trip.

Cooling off in Belize, back in the hair days.

I caught a bus to the Caribbean coast, which at the time was even less developed and populated than the rest of the country. There were grubby, unsafe towns followed by quaint little villages as one went further and further away from the main populated areas. It was wildly exotic to me as I looked out of the bus, but once I caught a boat down the coastal river, it was another world altogether.

The boat trip was an all-day adventure through the rainforest which, up until now, I had only seen in books and documentaries. There were sloths and toucans in the trees and countless iguanas of all sizes crawling on the banks and in the branches hanging overhead.

I was let off in a village called Tortuguero and secured a simple room with a bunk and an outdoor shower. I had a simple dinner with some German tourists that I had met on the boat, sampled the local firewater called Guaro, and then went to bed. Tomorrow would be a big day.

The next morning involved getting a crash course in rainforest hiking from a local expert. He gave me a brief lesson about avoiding hazards, getting drinking water from vines, and finding direction under the canopy. After this very basic overview, I was given access to a traditional dugout canoe carved from a log, and was on my own.

I followed the instruction of the local guide and pointed my canoe in the direction of a dimly visible tributary across the river. He recommended that I paddle slightly upstream as I crossed so that the gentle current would carry me right into it, where lots of wildlife could be sighted. I went along with this and was surprised out how easily mastered the dugout was my first time out.

Just as the guide predicted, gathering some natural momentum as I crossed made everything easier once I made it two thirds of the way and turned the canoe. It was now just a matter of pointing the craft toward the confluence and being gently carried into the stream by the force of the larger river.

Basiliscus plumifrons

As beautiful and mysterious as the village and its surrounding forest were, this little stream was otherworldly. It was completely still and without current, more of a narrow

YOU'RE GONNA' GET BIT

bayou, and completely shaded by an overhead canopy of trees. It was like paddling through a dark tunnel.

The noises of the rainforest came alive as I made my way through. The buzzing insects welcomed me, but the loudest voices were yet to come. Ten minutes downstream, howler monkeys began their chorus and leapt from tree to tree. These were surprisingly difficult to spot and photograph with the poor light and their quick, fleeting appearances.

This short excursion upstream provided a feast for anyone interested in reptiles and amphibians. Inside of two hours I was able to view many of my favorite exotic species that I had been fascinated by since childhood.

A beautifully plumed male *Basiliscus plumifrons* (Green basilisk) was perched at the end of a protruding branch right in front of my canoe before darting classically across the stream on its rear legs to safety.

....
77

I parked the canoe on a bank and took a brief walk on land. Not five minutes into the jungle I found a juvenile *Bothriechis schlegelii* (eyelash viper) showing off its brilliant yellow coloration as it reclined in the crotch of a tree.

Bothriechis schlegelii

The prize of the day belonged to my discovery on the way back to the lodge after turning around in the tributary. Looking into a small backwater, I found a six-foot wild cousin of Rocco! He pretended not to see me as I paused and enjoyed him from a respectful distance before heading back to the lodge.

I would save up for another year and take a similar trip to Belize. In addition to more herp encounters, I enjoyed some amazing snorkeling, Mayan ruins and camping in the national jaguar refuge. I saw everything I could see in that little country that my little Suzuki Samurai rental could get me to.

I am straying from the theme of this book a bit on these adventures. There is no harrowing tale to be told, just examples of amazing treks that were my pleasure to experience. It seems I was meant to encounter my hazards and dangers much closer to home.

Wild *Caiman crocodilus*

Life back at official adulthood included many dates, many houseguests, and several girlfriends. Most of this time was some of the best and most fun of my life. Yes, most of it.

One girlfriend in particular was none too happy when the relationship ended. I chose to

move on with life and she was having none of
it. Somehow during the all-to dramatic ending,
a call was placed to animal control.

It seems that spectacled caimans were not
completely welcome as far as the city was concerned. A young animal control officer ended
up knocking at my door. In fact, my landlord,
who lived in the home in front of me, was nice
enough to show the officer the way.

I was not exactly sure what was in store for
my life at this point. I brought the officer to the
extra room, and showed him the closet that I
had converted to an enclosure. By now Rocco
was well over four feet long. I prepared for my
arrest.

No arrest occurred, however. Instead I
shared some stories and chuckles with the officer and answered all of his questions. Still,
Rocco would have to go. The problem was that
the young, green officer was not quite up to the
task. This was all new territory for him.

He was happy to know that I would be doing all of the work for him. I figured that my
landlord must be concerned, and that the best
way through this was to be helpful and get the
officer on his way as soon as possible. It was
inevitable that Rocco was going. More backup
vehicles and officers would only draw more

attention to what could be a serious lease/law violation.

I picked up Rocco, explaining to the officer how it's done as I did so. We walked together to the animal control vehicle, the officer opened the holding container door, and I placed Rocco inside. I remember asking about what would happen next for all concerned, and not getting much in the way of helpful information.

The officer left. I waited and wondered. Minutes, hours and days went by with no eviction or even a question from the landlord. No tickets came in the mail and no prosecution was forthcoming. This problem, at least for me, was over.

I would see Rocco one last time in my life. I visited him at the animal control facility where he was waiting in the same type of enclosure that dogs were kept in. I was horrified at the sight and at the predicament I had put him in. What would happen to him?

The information I received was that I would not be getting Rocco back, not with the housing that I could provide and in the county that I resided. The workers were curt and to the point with me, as was deserved. They did, however, choose to reveal a bit of information about his destination.

It seems there was a private citizen living inland, outside of the city limits, who had facilities on his property for crocodilians. In fact they were of zoo quality, complete with large water pools and naturalistic land areas. He had set these facilities up years ago and was grandfathered into any changes in the law. Apparently he was a trusted last resort for such needs that the local zoo could not, or would not provide.

Feeling ashamed, amateurish, and rather irresponsible, I took solace in all of this. Rocco was getting larger and growing faster. I had always been able to provide him with good housing and plenty of food and light. He was fat and healthy, but his enclosure was beginning to seem unnatural. He may not have cared a bit, but it didn't look right.

I said my final goodbyes to Rocco through the bars of Animal Control's enclosure. I was not given any further information and would not be permitted to visit him at his future home. He was mine no more.

Other than not getting ahead of the problem, and not having the means to do better for him sooner, I have no regrets. Crocodilians live long lives. I have no doubt that he is alive today. If I had been at the point in my life then that I am now, I could have kept him in a suitable custom enclosure in my home. Distractions and poor choices of youth made things go another way.

It should be obvious now that I was in need of a break from large reptile keeping. I had a career to focus on and there was the fun of my twenties to have. I would still have some animals in my life, and for some reason there was a five-year period or so that I had a bird, but that is quite another story.

I still had a good selection of aquariums at my disposal. I took an interest in tropical fish and smaller amphibians which utilized these. I also was a go between for people that needed to re-home a variety of reptiles over the years, including turtles, large iguanas and boa constrictors. I would never get attached again, however, and would eventually find more enthusiastic new keepers to sell them to.

Part V

Going Pro

Life transitions took place. I got married, became a father and was occupied by home improvement projects. This was a suburban life void of fun in the field, working unrelated jobs, and precious little time for things herp. Only a pet turtle and modest tropical fish setup darkened my door for a good six years or so.

A drastic move would change this interruption in the reptile and amphibian world for me. Southern California real estate prices were going bonkers. We ended up selling all of our property and moving to coastal Texas in a whirlwind decision.

Where we were almost never at the beach in California, we now could visit any time we wished from a nice home, minutes away. Our home buying dollars went much further in this market, but there was one problem. Very few jobs in my field of expertise at the time could be found in this area.

This meant down time. It was kind of a nice semi-retirement of setting up a new home and gulf fishing for a while. Eventually, though, I would have to return to the workplace.

A job relating to previous work I had done in graphic design was available. I interviewed and received an offer! Not two weeks into the new position, the bloom was off the rose. I quickly hated the job with every fiber of my being; in fact I believed that I was working for a semi-crooked outfit. It was the only job I had ever quit without notice, leaving the same day - like they do in the movies!

This was a liberating move for me, but it rang hollow after a few weeks of no paycheck. Whittling away at my savings was not the purpose behind this move. I was becoming a bit frustrated.

A couple of months went by. I occupied my time with remodeling a fixer-upper and a rental property. Still, a regular paycheck would be needed, so I devoted much additional time to filling out applications and searching ads.

During one regular search of the Sunday paper, a particular ad stood out. A local institution had a snake venom research program and was looking for a web designer and marketing specialist. Web design *and* reptiles!

This opportunity had my full attention. I was able to schedule an interview, but was apprehensive. Surely, I assumed, there would be many qualified applicants for a job like this. The interview went well as far as interviews go. I left cautiously optimistic but continued in my job hunt.

YOU'RE GONNA' GET BIT

As it turns out, there was something about the combination of skills and my background with reptiles and amphibians that they liked. In particular, they noted my published articles in a popular aquarium hobbyist magazine that I had written years prior. This went far with the scientific writing tasks associated with the position.

I received an offer and took it immediately. It would be a very different setting from what I had done for a living for the past ten years, but I was more than ready for something new.

The research facility was equipped with the latest laboratory equipment and had a collection of hundreds of venomous snakes. I would be in charge of web development and writing articles for the institution.

My writing and web design duties, however, would be second in priority in short order. The institution underwent changes with the individual doing venom extraction and managing the snake facility. Eventually the director took over the snake milking duties, but he was looking for a more permanent solution.

He asked if I would be willing to try milking. I had absolutely no experience with venomous snakes. I had never handled one, never caught one, and had never even seen one in the wild except for one that we ran over during a boar hunting trip in Monterrey. So of course I would be willing to try.

I started training on two different types of non-venomous snakes. One was a *Masticophis flagellum testaceus* (Western coachwhip), the other was a *Pituophis catenifer sayi* (bullsnake). Both of them gave me a lot of trouble in completely different ways.

The coachwhip went ballistic as soon as the tong grabbers were placed on him by my extraction partner. The snake then did his best to get his mouth at me as he thrashed about. Following the guidance of the director, I was able to get him under control with the pinning stick, grab him from behind the head, and take control of his body with my other hand. I then was able to bring him over for a mock biting of the parafilm-wrapped sample cup.

The bull snake was longer, bulkier and stronger. He also didn't much care for being grabbed, and in addition to thrashing, wrapped himself around my arm once I had him. I took this all in stride and again brought him to the cup for imaginary milking.

The tricky part would be in unraveling his body from my arm as I kept control of the head. If I were to simply release the snake onto the extraction table or back into the cage, he could remain attached to me and bite at will. This was good practice for snakes such as cobras, which commonly wrap themselves around the arm during extraction.

Both practice milkings went well. At this point, after a fresh success, there was no reason to wait in trying the real thing. A new cup was prepared with fresh parafilm stretched on top. We carefully selected from our specimens so that if indeed there was an accident, at least it would involve a species whose venom is *least* toxic.

The specimen chosen was a medium-sized *Agkistrodon contortrix contortrix* (Southern copperhead). Apparently if one is going to be bitten by a venomous snake, this is the one to choose. Fantastic!

This is not to say that being bitten by a copperhead will not ruin one's day. It most certainly will. There will be tremendous pain, swelling and a definite hospital visit. There is a very high probability of surviving a copperhead bite and even having no permanent damage to limbs or digits, but it will change your plans for the day.

After gearing myself up, I was ready for venomous snake number one. The director grabbed the snake with tongs and it thrashed about angrily as he pulled it from the cage. I took a good look at the situation from all angles with my pin stick ready. It was time to make my move.

I found my target and quickly but gently pinned the snake's head down from behind the head. Pausing briefly to be sure of my hold, I then went in with my right hand, grabbed, and controlled the head with my index finger.

I was expecting all hell to break loose, but that didn't happen. In fact, the snake was much less hostile than the previous two that I had practiced with. Sure, the consequences of a mistake were grave, but it was a nice feeling to know that the struggle experienced was at a lesser degree than expected.

I took hold of the body and announced "Got it!" and had the snake completely under control. From here it was brought to the cup where it willingly bit and produced a milliliter of venom for our inventory.

There was still the matter of depositing the snake back to the cage. There is the choice of releasing it onto the table where an assistant could grab it with tongs and place it into the cage. Another option is to simply place it into the cage and, with a slight toss, pull the hands away and shut the cage door all in one fluid motion.

I decided that I had come this far without a hitch, so I may as well experience the entire process. I moved him into the cage, made certain that no part of the body was wrapped around my arm, and tossed him in. The most startling part of the experience was the slamming of the sliding door followed by the thrashing of the snake, but the handling went exceedingly well. I was ready for more.

There was no break. I didn't want one. I wanted to keep the rhythm going and not take the chance of becoming hesitant or second guessing myself. I continued on with more copperheads, *Agkistrodon piscivorus leucostoma* (Western Cottonmouth), *Crotalus ruber* (Red Diamond Rattlesnake) and an average sized *Crotalus atrox* (Western Diamondback Rattlesnake).

We stopped after extractions from twenty snakes of various species of North America. All of them, without exception, gave me less of a hard time than did the non-venomous practice snakes. Not only was my trial by fire successful, but I was now officially taking over as the new snake venom extractor.

I ended up taking over some managerial duties at the snake house over the next year as well. I was very much enjoying my work and the experience I had gained, but some circumstances at home required me to make a tough decision.

I made a brief detour in my snake career in order to be closer to my son's school. He has autism and at times one of us parents would be needed to help him during the day. I would take a new position that closely tied to my previous marketing work, but most importantly, it was a short ride from my home and paid slightly more. The job in snake venom research was an hour commute away.

I made an effort to make the best of a position that I didn't enjoy for two years. When I discovered that there was an opening for a serpentarium manager back at the institution, however, I applied and hoped that I would be forgiven for leaving. I was taken back, this time to an even better position. I fully embraced making a living in the herp world again.

I was suddenly the curator of an entire serpentarium of five hundred venomous snakes, and I wasn't even a snake guy. As it turns out, however, being a snake guy is not what is needed to succeed at this job. The primary goal, for both you and your employees, is not getting bit.

A bite in this line of work is frowned upon and becomes a big hassle. There is the protocol of grabbing suitable antivenom, followed by alerting the director, then being driven to the hospital and staying for an undetermined amount of days. Once one is feeling better, there is all manner of paperwork to be completed and negative attention to the program. Getting bit is better avoided. Avoid it I did.

After a couple of months I was to receive my first delivery of venomous snakes from a private collector in Arizona named Dave. He had a load of fifteen rattlesnakes of different species and brought them packed in individual pillow cases placed in a larger plastic container.

He was an experienced naturalist in the field, whereas I was only experienced with handling and extracting from captive specimens. Thankfully, I am now aware of techniques to wrap and unwrap venomous snakes from their pillow cases that I didn't know then.

I started grabbing pillow cases willy-nilly as I did with the ball pythons that came in similar packaging so many years back. I picked them up and started working on the knots as the contents rattled at their awakening. The donor watched me with concern until he had enough.

"Brother, you're gonna' get bit." Dave said calmly. I altered my method a bit at hearing this and changed my grip on the pillow case. I felt instant embarrassment at looking like an amateur in front of a new colleague, but I was very willing to listen.

He cautioned me about handling cloth containers, describing how brushing up against them could easily result in a bite through the material. This should have been obvious to me but now I know. I was certainly grateful to receive the warning and remain incident free.

Dave also provided an ominous warning about my profession in general. "When you work with venomous snakes, at some point you're gonna' get bit." I have decided to avoid this prediction after twenty thousand snake milkings, even while realizing that it could happen tomorrow.

I have always had an odd feeling that if and when I get bit, it will be in the breeding room. The breeding room is technically referred to as a "hibernaculum", as this is where we bring certain snakes to induce an artificial dormant state. Once they have chilled in fifty-five degree temperatures for a few months, they are brought back up to eighty degrees, fed well, and then paired for breeding.

It is in the pairing that things tend to get tricky for me. I am on the wrong side of forty now so I can be forgetful. During the course of daily maintenance one becomes accustomed to working with one snake per cage. During the breeding days, however, snakes get doubled up.

This is where one particular incident illustrates the dangers of that combination of hazards. I was in the hibernaculum making some annual pairings of select individuals. One particular pair was *Crotalus scululatus* (Mojave rattlesnake). The venom of this snake is highly toxic, and bite victims can be hit with both hemotoxic and neurotoxic effects to tissue and the nervous system. Not the snake on the short list of those to have an accident with.

I opened a large cage that was placed on a shelf at mid-body level. This cage housed two mojaves that we were hoping would become acquainted. Doing some routine maintenance, I removed the male, placed it into the temporary holding container and turned to grab a microchip reader in order to verify the individual specimen number.

I fumbled with the reader a bit and lost my train of thought. I then dropped a pen that decided to roll across the floor. Distracted and bending over to chase the pen, I turned my body around and lost concentration. I retrieved the pen and rose back up to continue. I looked up to see the female, now at the wide open cage door, staring me in the face.

This was a brief stare down. I remember seeing her flickering tongue and her body coiling slowly. She did not seem to be agitated or feeling threatened in any way, as she was not rattling much. Still, the proximity of my face to hers was a matter of inches. I did not freeze for long and quickly backed away as far as I could, which was not very far in such cramped quarters. It was enough to get away with a warning, and I have been extra cautious in that room ever since.

Having gone through these close calls, I felt that I was armed with the knowledge required for most of what could happen. I went on to do daily venom extractions and maintenance tasks without a hitch. Over the next year I was feeling more and more confident in my abilities, and managing the facility was going well.

Every morning I have a routine where I inspect the snake rooms. Each room holds approximately one hundred snakes. I start with the room closest to the front of the building by pulling out my master key, opening the door, flipping the light switches and entering. I then inspect cages to check on the overall well-being of the specimens.

On one sleepy Monday morning, I was yawning through the normal routine. I went through each room and found no unusual issues as expected. I then came to room number three and opened the door.

Opening the door and reaching for the light switch is almost done in one motion. The second hand is close behind and already reaching, in order to have light as soon as possible. There is always one rack of snake cages situated closest to the door compared to the rest, maybe a foot and a half away from the entrance.

This morning the closest rack was there as usual. Wrapped around the rack support bar, however, staring at me was one of our *Naja pallida* (red spitting cobras). I let out a tremendous "Holy (F-WORD)!" and boy was I awake now.

There is no freezing or slowly backing away in a situation as this. There is only backing up and closing the door if you are fortunate enough to have one. I did this, allowed my heart to recover, and reassessed my morning routine for this particular room.

I cursed the name of one if my employees, assuming that he had cleaned the cage of this cobra, got distracted, and forgot to return him from the temporary holding container back into his proper cage.

I would have to deal with him when his shift started later. Now I had a snake out of place that needed to be wrangled. Fortunately, we had snake tongs, snake hooks and containers of all types and sizes located in just about every room in the facility. I returned to the previous room to select a four-foot tong grabber, a long hooking stick and a pair of goggles.

The name "spitting cobra" is rather intimidating. Fortunately I was dealing with captive-born specimens that rarely utilize this defense. Nevertheless, precautions need to be taken. They never seem to spit at their captors until they do.

The main challenge would be in unwrapping his body from the cage rack that he had comfortably entangled himself into. With my goggles on and tools ready, I opened the door again.

The fright of him being out of place was subsiding and he cooperated with being handled and placed into a temporary container as well as these things will cooperate.

The reason he was placed into a temporary holding container was the same reason he was outside of his home in the first place. Looking at his normal enclosure, it became obvious that a freak accident had occurred.

Some of our larger cages were put together utilizing a sliding glass pane inserted into a track for front access and viewing. The track is set into the cage with glue. As it turns out, this glue can corrode and fail over a number of years, and the glass panel may simply pop out. A little encouragement from an active and probing animal like a cobra can accelerate the process.

This was all quite evident as I looked over at the formerly secure cage with shattered glass all over the floor. I was relieved to know that my employee was not to blame. We would, however, have another variable to discuss at our next safety meeting.

This was another catastrophe avoided and another lesson learned. Over the years there would be countless daily hazards to contend with, as will always be so in this line of work.

A common question I get is why I am not wearing protective gloves or a suit of armor when extracting venom. My philosophy on handling venomous snakes is to have all of

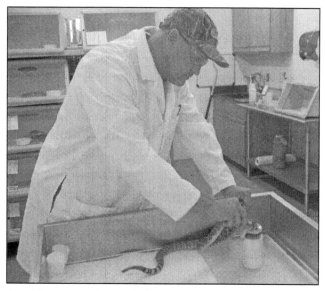

Extracting venom from *Crotalus atrox*

one's physical assets available to operate uninhibited. Any restriction of movement or sense of touch would dull my interpretation of what the animal is doing or about to do.

If I am grabbing the back of a snake's head with a thick glove, I will not be able to feel minor twitches that are clues to what the snake will do next. If I am grabbing a caiman by the body with heavy gloves on, my grip will not be its tightest and again, will not feel subtle warnings of when the animal may burst into a struggle.

Of course with popular nature/reality shows nowadays, the extreme in the other direction is often encouraged. I avoid all unnecessary handling done in unnecessary ways.

For example, I have seen handlers on television grabbing a venomous snake by the tail and then lifting it into the air while controlling the head with a snake tool. This is shown as the "professional" way to handle snakes yet it usually serves no purpose other than good TV.

A large percentage of all venomous snake bites occur in situations where people are handling them unnecessarily. As counterintuitive as it may seem to mess with a venomous snake, the appeal of the risk is magnetic for some. Statistics have shown the usual scenarios to involve males and/or alcohol consumption combined with a daredevil mentality. This is something most of us fellas have inside of us to some degree.

My suspicion has always been that another factor involved is the novelty and unusual nature of a venomous snake sighting. For the average person, including me, encountering one in the outdoors is quite rare.

Let's look at a scenario of the snake encounter by any group of people. A rattlesnake is spotted near the family campsite or the daily jobsite. Rattlesnake! Rattlesnake! Everyone must be alerted to this rare encounter with a dangerous creature, everyone must rush to provide aid or observe, and finally, everyone must be protected from it. That is where the hero comes in.

This hero has a yearning to go above and beyond. He acquires a stick or other tool and gets to work. If lucky, he kills the snake right away. Many times, however, he is tempted to move it, raise it up in the air to take pictures, or even attempt to pin the head.

It is in this urge to manipulate the snake in some way that people get bit. Now that everyone owns digital cameras or a phone with camera, I expect these types of occurrences to continue and increase.

The bottom line is that venomous snake bite statistics are highly affected by the "Watch this!" and "Watch me!" part of our character that often has unpleasant consequences.

I can say that I only have motivation to put my hands on venomous snakes because I am paid to do so, and know that any accidents will be paid for by my employer. Venomous snake bite treatments are horrendously expensive!

The type of person that is indifferent and unimpressed by snake handling is the ideal candidate to handle them for a living, and that is why I am paid to do so. Thrill-seekers need not apply, and hobbyists can be too enamored with the animals in some cases. Mine is a more clinical approach, and seems to have served me well thus far.

As a separate part of my job, I am occasionally called on to retrieve snakes from homes and businesses in the community. One call that stands out as particularly interesting occurred on a spring morning after a two-day stretch of rainy days. A woman was hearing a rattle in her back porch, and feared that her cat may have been bitten.

My co-worker and I gathered snake sticks and buckets and were on our way to a semi-rural residence less than one quarter mile from our facility. Seconds after turning on the street of the residence we were called to, I slammed on the brakes at the sight of a *Micrurus tener* (Texas coral snake) crossing the street!

The house call would have to wait. We busted out of the vehicle with our tools and raced after the snake which was moving at quite a clip to get out of the road. The snake crawled into a storm drain with an iron grate over it. I lifted the grate as my partner fished into the drain to catch the coral snake.

The grate slipped from my hands and almost crushed the fingers of my co-worker. This would not have reflected well on our competence if things went a different way, with him sent to the hospital with broken fingers. I was again spared for my screw-up and we managed to get the snake into a bucket.

Back in the vehicle and making our way down the street, we were on to the original destination. Police vehicles and the lady of the house were anxiously awaiting our arrival. It seems the woman had some sway in the community.

Fortunately I always keep a spare bucket in the back of my Jeep in case of a call. It had to be dumped of its contents of auto parts and emergency items of course, but it was quite usable.

We explained the fascinating detour we took to catch the coral snake, but the woman was ready to have her own snake issue out of her life. We went to the back yard where she pointed out the spot where the rattling noise was coming from. There was a large tarp covering some lawn equipment being stored closely beside the house.

After poking around the area it would not be long before we heard the rattling. We pinpointed the sound as best we could and lifted the tarp. My partner went in with the grabber to pick up one huge Western Diamondback. I was bringing him the bucket with the lid ready when he added "There's two of them!"

It seems we had one resting right atop another. They would have to share the same bucket on the way back to the facility as the second bucket was accounted for by the coral snake.

This is an example of one of the more unusual calls I've been on. Three venomous snakes within the span of ten minutes! The two Westerns were among the largest we had acquired from a local residence. Less than a year later, the woman called once again stating that there was a "huge" rattlesnake in her yard.

Normally we take the description of "huge" lightly, but in her case we will always take it quite literally. This time around the snake was even larger and not even ten steps away from the spot snakes were found just months before.

There is certainly something about her home and its surroundings that they fancy.

On another snake pickup, I had to retrieve a Texas coral snake found at the local botanical gardens. Folks are usually in a hurry to have someone come and get these things, so I quickly grabbed the first container I could find and was on my way.

The pickup went very well. I exchanged the usual banter with the donors, transferred the snake from their container to mine, and put it in the truck for the ride back to work. I picked my radio station and drove on down the road. Easy!

The problem arose when arriving at work. I picked up the container again, which was made of transparent plastic, and saw nothing inside.

I opened up the lid and realized what had happened. A crack had formed in the plastic and a corner of the container broke off, creating a gap. It wasn't a large gap, but was just enough for the coral snake to exploit and free itself. Coral snakes are notorious and talented escape artists.

Coral snakes are not a very aggressive snake, but are highly toxic. They inject a neurotoxin that can cause neuromuscular dysfunction and in extreme cases, heart failure. The symptoms can be quite delayed after a bite and then progress suddenly and rapidly.

What I could not stop thinking about was that these snakes love to crawl into tight hiding places. So where was the snake? I first checked my boots, then my pants (wouldn't you?). After multiple neurotic checks, I was satisfied that it didn't make its way into my clothing.

I then began the process of looking under every seat, every accessible piece of carpet and everything not bolted down. There was no snake to be found.

It would be a week before my wife could set foot in my truck. She finally felt convinced that it was safe because of the smell of death permeating the entire vehicle. It would be another two weeks before all traces of that were gone.

Somewhere deep in the intricate workings of the truck dashboard, I thought, a Texas coral snake skeleton will eventually be found. Three years later I dismantled the dash to fix a broken evaporator coil, but I never did find the remains. Perhaps the next lucky chap to own the truck will have better luck.

I'm quite fortunate to make a living in this fascinating way. I'm also privileged to be able to go on annual snake collection trips in the field. Thus far I have been hunting venomous snakes mostly in the desert Southwest and West Texas.

A short list of species comes to mind as an example of reptiles and amphibians encountered during both official collecting trips and my personal expeditions in the field:

- *Crotalus molossus* (Black-tailed Rattlesnake)
- *Crotalus oreganus oreganus* (Northern Pacific Rattlesnake)
- *Nerodia rhombifer* (Diamondback Water Snake)
- *Thamnophis marcianus* (Checkered Garter Snake)
- *Bogertophis subocularis* (Trans-Pecos Rat Snake)
- *Elaphe obsoleta lindheimerii* (Texas Rat Snake)
- *Drymarchon Corais erebennus* (Texas Indigo Snake)
- *Leptotyphlops dulcis* (Texas Blind Snake)
- *Aspidoscelis sexlineata* (Six-lined Racerunner)
- *Hemidactylus tursicus* (Mediterranean Gecko)
- *Alligator mississippiensis* (American Alligator)
- *Lepidochelys kempii* (Kemp's Ridley Sea Turtle)
- *Gopherus berlandieri* (Texas Tortoise)
- *Trachemys scripta elegans* (Red-eared Slider)
- *Gopherus agassizii* (Desert Tortoise)
- *Apalone spinifera emoryi* (Texas spiny softshell turtle)
- *Hyla cinerea* (Green Tree Frog)
- *Gastrophryne olivacea* (Great Plains Narrow-mouthed Toad)

I expect the list to grow as my missions laid out by the institution expand to other areas. It will grow regardless of the way I make my living.

I will always enjoy the natural world and the new and exciting encounters with animals that it provides. I'm privileged to have a role in the discovery of biomedical applications through the specimens I collect and the samples that I extract and process. It all started with my childhood fascination with reptiles and amphibians. The encounters and stories promise to continue through my life.

YOU'RE GONNA' GET BIT

Epilogue

I waited as long as possible to write an update on the dire predictions of my occupation. At the time of final edits, I have performed well over 25,000 extractions from venomous snakes. I continue with daily extractions and have not been bit.

YOU'RE GONNA' GET BIT

Photos

Propelling the dugout canoe in Costa Rica (early 90's)

4wd rental in Belize. Never got stuck!

YOU'RE GONNA' GET BIT

West Texas snake country

First *Crotalus atrox* wild capture

YOU'RE GONNA' GET BIT

First breeding success! Albino and typical *Crotalus atrox*

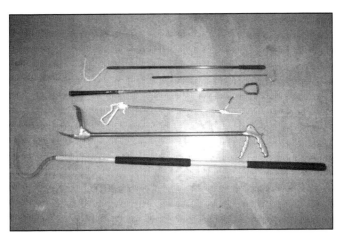

Some tools of the venomous snake handling trade

YOU'RE GONNA' GET BIT

Hyla cinerea

My only home herp project these days. Raising *Notophthalmus viridescens*.

Mark Ferdinand

Mark Ferdinand lives on the South Texas coast with his wife, daughter and son. Fishing the surf, hunting, gardening, tiki carving, auto and home repair occupy his spare time. He has written on the topic of autism spectrum disorder from a father's perspective in parenting articles and in other non-fiction venues.

Having limited typical communication skills, his son introduced Mark to new ways of interpreting his needs and aspirations. As his son grew older Mark became fascinated by the story potential within these amazing children. This prompted the creation of a dynamic adventure story focusing on a character with autism, Fortune on the Spectrum.

After completing his first novel, Mark decided to compile a group of lifetime reptile and amphibian stories that brought him to such an unusual line of work in snake venom extraction.

Books by Mark Ferdinand

Autism and Fatherhood
Fortune on the Spectrum – An Adventure Novel
You're Gonna' Get Bit!

Bachelor on the Spectrum (Coming 2016-2017)

42725653R00083

Made in the USA
San Bernardino, CA
10 December 2016